STO

FRIENDS
OF ACPL

W9-CMI-125

IS THIS MY DINNER?

IRMA SIMONTON BLACK

Pictures by Rosalind Fry

ALBERT WHITMAN & Company, Chicago

Library of Congress Cataloging in Publication Data

Black, Irma (Simonton) 1906–
    Is this my dinner?

    SUMMARY: A youngster looking for his dinner
discovers several kinds of food he cannot eat.
    [1. Stories in rhyme.   2. Food—Fiction]
I. Fry, Rosalind, illus.   II. Title.
PZ8.3.B57Is   [E]   72–83682
ISBN 0–8075–3665–2

Second Printing 1977

Text © Copyright 1972 in name of The Estate of Irma Simonton Black
Illustrations © Copyright 1972 by Rosalind Fry
Published simultaneously in Canada by George J. McLeod, Limited, Toronto
Lithographed in the U.S.A.   All rights reserved

Books by
Irma Simonton Black

DOCTOR PROCTOR
AND MRS. MERRIWETHER

THE LITTLE OLD MAN
WHO COULD NOT READ

THE LITTLE OLD MAN
WHO COOKED AND CLEANED

2091150

I'm hungry!
I want my dinner!

Is this my dinner? Hay?
A pile of hay?
No! No! I say.
All that hay so brown and coarse—
that is dinner for a—

Yes, that is dinner for a horse.
And here he is!

Is this my dinner?
A knobby bone?
That's nothing that I want to own.
Then who's it for?
Who's running up?

A wagging, panting,
bouncy pup.

Is this my dinner on the ground?
All these acorns, hard and round?
No, no, I say.
Take them away.
That's not food
for boys or girls.
But here they come—

—the hungry squirrels.
They'll eat them.

Is this my dinner?
A wiggly worm?
Just thinking of it makes me squirm.
I won't eat it.
But I've heard
that someone will—

–a hungry bird.

Is this my dinner?
An ear of corn, all hard and dry,
is something I don't want to try!
It's no food that I would pick.
It's dinner for—

Yes, dinner for a little chick.

Is this my dinner?
Melon rinds and apple peels?
I can think of better meals.

But fruit peels little, fruit peels big
taste good to—look!—a hungry pig.
He grunts and snuffs—

—and gobbles them up!

Is this my dinner?
This small raw fish?
To me that's not a tasty dish.
But I know someone small and furry
who runs to eat it, glad and purry.

My kitty.

2091150

Is grass my dinner? It's green and sweet,
but better to roll upon than eat.
There's something eating grass right now—
do you see—

Yes, you can see a big brown cow.
She likes it.

Is this my dinner?
Milk and meat,
vegetables and something sweet?

Yes, yes! That's mine, exactly right!
Now watch me, I'll eat every bite.

See?